CAN THE CHURCH
MAKE IT?

YOUTH FORUM SERIES

Titles in Print

YF1 YOUTH ASKS, WHY BOTHER ABOUT GOD?
  by Alvin N. Rogness

YF2 YOUTH CONSIDERS SEX
  by William E. Hulme

YF3 YOUTH CONSIDERS "DO-IT-YOURSELF" RELIGION
  by Martin E. Marty

YF4 YOUTH CONSIDERS PARENTS AS PEOPLE
  by Randolph C. Miller

YF5 YOUTH CONSIDERS PERSONAL MOODS
  by Reuel L. Howe

YF6 YOUTH CONSIDERS MARRIAGE
  by David R. Mace

YF7 YOUTH CONSIDERS DOUBT AND FRUSTRATION
  by Paul L. Homer

YF8 YOUTH ASKS, WHAT'S LIFE FOR?
  by D. T. Niles

YF9 YOUTH ASKS, DOES GOD STILL SPEAK?
  by Andrew M. Greeley

YF10 YOUTH ASKS, IS GOD A GAME?
  by Normal C. Habel

YF11 SCIENCE AND FAITH—TWIN MYSTERIES
  by William G. Pollard

YF12 PRAYER—WHO NEEDS IT?
  by Annette Walters

YF13 LET'S FACE RACISM
  by Nathan Wright, Jr.

YF14 IS THIS TRIP NECESSARY?
  by Philip and Lola Deane

YF15 THE WAITING GAME
  by Roy W. Fairchild

YF16 THE INFORMATION EXPLOSION
  by William Kuhns

YF17 YOU WANT TO CHANGE THE WORLD?
  SO CHANGE IT!
  by Paul Simon

YF18 WHEN I DON'T LIKE MYSELF
  by William E. Hulme

YF19 IS GOD FOR REAL?
  by Peter A. Bertocci

YF20 APPOINTMENT WITH DEATH
  by Alvin N. Rogness

YF21 WHAT ABOUT HOMOSEXUALITY?
  by Clinton R. Jones

YF22 WHAT ABOUT THE OCCULT—FAKE OR FAITH?
  by Thomas J. Kiresuk

YF23 CAN THE CHURCH MAKE IT?
  by Elmer N. Witt

CREATIVE WAYS TO USE YOUTH FORUM BOOKS
  by Clarence E. Nelson

A YOUTH FORUM BOOK

CAN THE CHURCH MAKE IT?

by

Elmer N. Witt

THOMAS NELSON INC.
Nashville / Camden / New York

ISBN: 0–8407–5322–5
Library of Congress Catalog Card Number: 75–5252

Printed in the United States of America

FOREWORD

This book is one of a series in a unique publishing effort in which Youth Research Center, Inc., Minneapolis, Minnesota, has joined with Thomas Nelson Inc., Nashville, Tennessee. The books are based on the very real concerns, problems, aspirations, searchings and goals of young people today as measured by nation-wide surveys being conducted continuously by the research center.

Central to the series is the belief that we all have a compelling need to turn to a core of faith for guidelines in coping with the world in which we live. Each book deals with a specific need or concern of young people viewed in relation to the Christian faith. By drawing upon the results of the surveys, each author is helped to speak more directly to the conflicts, values and beliefs of today's young people.

The significance of this series is enhanced, as well, by the scholarship and commitment of the authors. The grasp of the field in which each writes lends authority to their work and has established this series as a basic reference eagerly read and appreciated by young people.

INTRODUCTION

CAN THE CHURCH MAKE IT? is a presumptuous title. It sounds like there's an easy answer. Maybe "yes." Maybe "no." Like there is someone who really knows. Much of this book may sound authoritarian and paternalistic. That's one of the dangers of analysis.

In places it will sound as though I'm against all sorts of things . . . clergy, laity, preaching, church buildings, modern worship, traditional worship, apathetics, activists, and much more.

That's why I want to put my cards on the table. Criticism is easy, but that's not why this book was written. I really am looking for answers to the question: "Can the church make it?" I have some ideas, some feelings, some convictions about the church, that local gathering of Christian people. And a puzzling abundance of hope.

I will be trying to describe my ideas, feelings, and convictions, and I trust the hope will filter through.

It would be ridiculous to write for young people about the mission of the local church without being equally honest about the sad shape many local churches are in.

And *sad* is a carefully chosen word: unhappy, despondent, discouraged, deplorably bad.

I don't for one moment imagine that writing another book on the subject will change the situation drastically. Next to preaching, book-writing must be one of the least effective and satisfying of human efforts. This book is meant, rather, as an opportunity for us to stop, look, question, reflect, and talk about what a church is all about. Perhaps only those who share with me the unexplainable abundance of hope will bother to begin.

So inevitably, this is written for those who still care about those local gatherings and who still believe something can and should and does happen when people gather freely, purposefully, and honestly in the name of God.

A further point: you and I should have some understanding about the words I will be using. Many of them will be defined as they are used. By "church" I mean a local congregation of Christians, not a building or national denomination or world-wide communion of saints.

And "making it" means that local gathering being what it is meant to be, and doing what it is meant to do, and surviving as it is meant to survive. As much as possible, I have tried to let the One who started those gatherings of Christians define what it means to "make it."

A final point: when you write for others, you have to decide whether to use the third person, "he, they," or the first person, "I, we." This can be tricky in a book dealing with the objective situation (the way things are in our churches today) with the subjective (ideas, opinions and suggestions). As you will notice, I have used third person in the descriptive/analytical sections and first person in the subjective, even devotional parts.

I hope you don't mind shifting back and forth, but learning to shift gears may be one of the important lessons those local gatherings of Christians have to teach.

TABLE OF CONTENTS

Introduction   *vii*

1. It's Easy to Forget You Can Forget   *3*
2. God Unlimited   *7*
3. "According to Our Latest Survey"   *11*
4. In This Corner—The Clergy!   *17*
5. And in This Corner—The Laity   *23*
6. ". . . I Call You Friends"   *29*
7. Human Beings of God   *37*
8. Earth Is Not a Desert Drear   *43*
9. Frankly, the Odds Are Bad   *49*
10. Compromise Is not a Four-letter Word   *55*
11. Small Is Beautiful   *61*
12. Trustworthy Rather Than Predictable   *67*
    The Last Word   *73*

CAN THE CHURCH
MAKE IT?

1.

IT'S EASY
TO FORGET YOU CAN FORGET

"God, whom you will remember from our sermon last week . . ."

Comedian David Steinberg's line gets a quick laugh every time he uses it. The humor is built on the assumption that everyone remembers God. He does not have to be identified, certainly not to church people.

But the line makes us uneasy. The fact of the matter is that it *is* possible to forget God. And strange as it may seem, it is possible and even probable that church folk are most subject to this forgetfulness.

The very idea of religious people gathering in a certain spot with some regularity is at least partially built on the premise that it is possible to forget God. The reasoning is this: We get so involved with the things we do that we need a time and a place to remind one another that God is important.

Religious people forget that they can forget God, even as they gather to remind each other that God is important. The very process of organizing to remember God is deceptive. Assembling, talking, singing, praying, moving, and whatever else happens is real. God is abstract.

It's easy to substitute the reality of worship for the reality of remembering God.

Really remembering God is a powerful experience. It is more than saying words. It is dealing with God himself, in his mighty actions with people in times past, and in his continued mighty actions in the present. It is more than a mental process, for it calls upon God's power and presence for the living moment. Remembering God involves the rememberer with all he knows, wants, needs and hopes for in his life in God. This is worship in remembrance of him.

Another way to forget God is to trivialize him. Several decades ago a British pastor wrote an excellent book, *Your God is Too Small.* An updated version would be helpful today.

What does it mean to trivialize God? First, it means to associate God with things, events, and people that are unimportant to those who have gathered to remember God. He is trivialized when a suburban congregation talks about God in terms of another time and place, even another language.

God is trivialized in an inner city congregation when people pretend that bad housing, too little food, no jobs, and poor education are unimportant compared to reading the Bible, singing hymns, or praying.

God is trivialized in a mission church when, along with the Gospel, the sending churches also offer their own administration and culture as the gift of God.

When God is real and important to us, we don't think of him in terms of the 16th century or talk about him in terms of the 10th century, or even the first century. We talk about him in terms of right now, and we find words that make sense right now.

We trivialize God when we focus on the insignificant,

such as how we do things when we gather together. Caring enough to give the very best is not a bad guide in preparing for what people do in church. Doing things decently and in order has been a religious preoccupation for centuries. Settings and experiences that reach people as they are and where they are, are helpful. But the best and the worst in external form can become a substitute for the actual remembering of God.

Some congregations spend more time instructing their acolytes or preparing an organ prelude or making cupcakes for the coffee hour than they do in digging in to the reality of God in his relationship with men.

Trivializing God means calling him "God" and then trying to renovate him in terms of what kind of "god" people will buy. Some people change "gods" as they switch cars, and the God they end up with gets to look more and more like those people than what he's really like. Often enough, this "god" turns out to be American, white, middle-class, male and, of course, a member of the denomination of your choice.

It is possible to forget God, or to remember a god who only slightly resembles the God of Revelation; the God of Abraham, Isaac and Jacob, the God and Father of Jesus Christ.

In other words, "making it" in the local congregation is a question of substance and essence rather than a question of form or method. Practically, this means that a local gathering of Christian people has to be convinced about WHO is getting them together and WHY. Tradition has its role, but obviously, it's not enough. Good feelings, congeniality and friendship also are important reasons for gathering. Need has its place. But these are secondary to the question of WHO is the originator, source and focus of the group, and WHY the group has gathered.

This means that "making it" for the congregation is a matter of one's belief about the nature of God and his relationship with men, rather than a question of the nature of worship, a definition of the church, or the reliability of the Bible—important as these matters may be in certain circumstances. "Making it" for the local church means taking God on his terms, meeting him in his arena, accepting his out-side-of-us-ness, struggling with his completeness, being caught by his mercy.

Without realizing it, a great many church members gain the impression that God is some enormous, divine jigsaw puzzle. They imagine they get a piece of this enormous puzzle each week, and they hope that some day the pieces will fit together and they will be able to see God. In the meantime, they gather to worship a partial God.

God is hidden. That's true. He has not chosen to expose himself fully. Part of being God is his quality of being above and beyond. But he is not a jigsaw puzzle and man does not get pieces of him week by week. The truth is that man gets all of God or nothing of God. He gives himself to man or does not give himself to man. Man may not fully grasp what is happening between God and man. And surely man does not fully know what to do about the part of it he does grasp. But it doesn't help to think of God as coming in pieces. God is whole. And "making it" in the local congregation means responding to the whole of God given to the whole of man.

2.

✳✳✳✳✳✳✳✳✳✳✳✳✳✳✳✳✳✳✳✳✳✳✳✳✳✳✳✳✳✳✳✳✳✳✳✳

GOD UNLIMITED

"Making it" in the local congregation has to do with taking God as he comes, now. No filtering. No diluting. No down payment with ten easy installments. In other words, "let God be God," and get out of his way. Or better, get in with his way.

This means to accept the truth that God is in charge. Man likes God, but he does not like a God who's in charge. Man prefers God in easy doses, manageable degrees, and workable arrangements. Very likely the most serious impediment to the local congregation "making it," is the congregation's limiting, restricting, narrowing, confining, and restraining of God.

The message of the Son of God, Jesus Christ, is that "God *is* in charge." In Jesus' preaching and teaching he called this message "the kingdom of God." It was *the* central theme in his life. He announced the Good News from God: "The right time has come and the Kingdom of God is near!" Parable after parable seeks to make the message clear—God is in charge. Not only *will* he be in charge, as predicted in Jesus' story of the final judgment: "Come and receive the kingdom which has been prepared for you ever since the creation of the world." But God *is* in charge: the kingdom already exists. "It is God's spirit who gives me the power to drive out demons, which proves that the Kingdom of God has already come upon you."

This was not simply a back-drop for the life of Christ, nor merely a long-range goal. In deed and word Jesus Christ went about the renewal of the world in terms of God's original purpose for it. He demonstrated the kingly rule of God, the only One who has done God's will on earth as it is in heaven.

The people of his day were accustomed to religion and religious practitioners. That was not what was new about Jesus. The people were not unaware of religious fanatics. That was not Jesus' attraction or power. The people of his day had a healthy respect for tradition and history. But that was not Jesus' special appeal.

Jesus' uniqueness was his total commitment to God Unlimited. In every way God is in charge. Nothing escapes. Nothing is neglected.

A person is sick. Jesus calls on the power of God to interrupt the sickness. God is in charge.

A person dies. God is in charge and life is restored.

A person is trapped in meaninglessness and immorality. A cup of water becomes the occasion for God to move in with judgment and love.

People are tricked into arrogance through the age and rigidity of their religious exercises. God is in charge and cuts them to size with his preference for mercy rather than liturgical sacrifices.

Masses of people are hungry away from home and market. Food is provided. God is in charge.

Political pressure is applied. Christ answers: "You have authority over me only because it was given to you by God." God is in charge.

A storm fills grown men with fear. Jesus speaks the word of peace to the wind. God is in charge.

Jaded society erects class and racial barriers. Christ reaches out in love to cheats, whores, outcasts, political opportunists. God is in charge.

Friends begin to wonder if Christ is for real. He answers: "The lame can walk, the lepers are made clean, the deaf can hear, the dead are raised to life, and the Good News is preached to the poor." God *is* in charge.

Christ's teaching was marked with the authority of his Father, the unlimited, unrestricted, unconfined, unrestrained God with whom Jesus is one. To know this is to know the truth that makes us free, unlimited people responding to the love of unlimited God.

The Christian congregation today seldom reflects God Unlimited. Most of the time church people are known for their limitations, restrictions, and narrowness, such as being for certain kinds of people from certain kinds of background with certain kinds of income and certain kinds of beliefs.

The local congregation—or gathering—is limited when, unlike God, its members see their own group as an end in itself, rather than a means to letting God's rule be known among men.

The local gathering is limited when, unlike God, it focuses on the souls of human beings as something unrelated to their bodies, minds, and emotions.

The local gathering is limited when it assumes that one kind of "grace" is present in God's care of nature and another kind of "grace" in his acceptance, mercy and love for mankind.

The local gathering is limited when it emphasizes individual piety at the expense of social concern and action. Jesus pictures the Unlimited God as being seriously and primarily interested at the last judgment in how Christians have demonstrated that God also is in charge of those who are hungry, thirsty, alienated, naked, sick, and in prison.

The local gathering is limited when its members see areas of life as "secular," removed from the Lordship of Christ. Therefore they avoid seeing that God is in charge of how people earn their money, choose each other, resolve ideological differences between nations, treat natural resources and the environment, care for the aged, the retarded, the repressed, the unlovely, treat children, organize corporate structures, set prices, levy taxes, and choose their life's work and life styles.

And when the local gathering is limited, it is not making it with the unlimited God, who "decided to bring the *whole universe* back to himself." Through his Son's death, he made peace and "brought back to himself *all things,* both on earth and in heaven" so that "in union with him *all things* have their proper place."

God is in charge.

3.

✶✶✶✶✶✶✶✶✶✶✶✶✶✶✶✶✶✶✶✶✶✶✶✶✶✶✶✶✶✶✶✶✶✶✶✶✶

"ACCORDING TO
OUR LATEST SURVEY . . ."

But what *is* happening, then, in those local gatherings of Christian people? The answer is not easy. Perhaps each of us can only answer for the congregations we have known over a length of time.

Many things are happening. The pattern is varied. No one description fits. But if we are to believe only a tenth of what religious people have been saying to one another and to the world in print, there are identifiable trends.

The key to the trends is disappointment, dissatisfaction and disillusionment with what is happening in local congregations, at least if you take seriously some of the books on church renewal published in the past 10 years:

> *The Dilemma of Modern Belief*
> *The Noise of Solemn Assemblies*
> *Who's Killing the Church?*
> *The Comfortable Pew*
> *My People is the Enemy*
> *The Humiliation of the Church*
> *The Suburban Captivity of the Churches*
> *The Church Inside Out*

God's Frozen People
The Gathering Storm in the Churches
Second Chance for American Protestants
Rocking the Ark
The Enemy is Boredom

And there are more, most of them written by loyal followers taking seriously religion and the local gatherings of religious people. People trying to help, no less.

But what *is* being said, "according to our latest survey . . . ?"

The most obvious: church attendance, going down for years, continues to decline. A symbol is the nationwide report on a poll indicating that 75 per cent of those questioned felt that religion was losing its influence in national life.

Almost equally obvious: financial trouble mounts as contributions dwindle. This is caused by less people participating as well as by changing attitudes on church giving by those still active in local congregations.

Equally important, if not as obvious: conflict within the churches—local, regional and national—resulting from religious involvement in social issues. Some church members, emphasizing the practical, day-to-day effect of the Christian faith upon the world they see and know, are labeled "liberal." Others stressing traditional, more personal and individual benefits of the Christian faith, are called "conservative." The labels often harmonize with political, economic and psychological beliefs as well.

More destructive: indifference, apathy and disinterest. It is not only that "nothing works anymore"; for many church people nothing is worth working at. "What difference does it make?" and, "Who cares?" are the most frequent responses of the day. The most frequent adjective used in describing this indifference is "massive."

For a little more to think about, here are a few specifics from some of the more widely quoted studies and books. For instance, Milton Rokeach wrote a most critical article in *Psychology Today* entitled "Faith, Hope and Bigotry." He said that the data from his study suggests a "deeply imbedded" hypocrisy in many religiously-oriented people and in organized religious institutions.

A sociologist, Peter Berger, a faculty member of Rutgers University, New Brunswick, New Jersey, writes more sympathetically in *The Noise of Solemn Assemblies.** But he concluded that in the United States Christianity gets "fatally" mixed up with society, respectability and the American way of life. And in the final analysis, Berger said, religious people are innoculated with small doses of "Christianoid concepts and terminology" which make them immune to any real encounter with the Christian message.

A Dutch theologian, J. C. Hoekendijk, professor of missions at Union Theological Seminary, New York, examined Christian mission efforts and decided that the call to evangelism is usually an effort at institutional survival more than anything else. And the motivation is usually "nothing but a nervous feeling of insecurity."*

Organized religion "has been an extremely relevant force in the personal lives of most middle-class Americans,"* according to Andrew J. Young, executive vice president of the Southern Christian Leadership Conference, Atlanta, Georgia. He affirmed that it had helped

---

* Peter Berger, *The Noise of Solemn Assemblies.* Garden City: Doubleday, 1961. J. C. Hoekendijk, *The Church Inside Out.* Philadelphia: The Westminster Press, 1966. Quotation of Andrew J. Young is from an address he gave to a conference on "The Relevancy of Organized Religion—An Agenda for the Future," at Hudson, Wisconsin, October 6 to 8, 1969. Reported in *Unity Trends,* November 1, 1969, in an unsigned article, "The Relevancy of 'Organized Religion.' "

preserve the values of western culture, educated freed slaves, served as a "half-way house" for Irish and Italian minorities, preserved their identity for the Jews. But Young maintained that organized religion failed in its prophetic judgments on the culture and in its ministry of reconciliation between classes and races.

Richard E. Wentz,* educational director for the Office of Religious Affairs at Pennsylvania State University, suspects the validity of the local church will return, but with an "umbrella principle" allowing more freedom for differences among members. And, he says, "many if not all of the clergy of the coming institution" will earn their financial livelihood elsewhere.

Wentz carefully calls his comments "visions," but Mary McDermott Shideler,* a Boulder, Colorado, author, opts for what she sees as reality. A pastor may see his church members as "a flock," but the members do not. The teacher, housewife, salesman, student, electrician, are chiefly concerned with going about their daily tasks. "Some of them may feel . . . the presence of the church supporting their occupations. Many more, I suspect, feel directly sustained in their work by God but not as a congregation . . ."

Theodore H. Erickson,* executive of the Board of Homeland Ministries, United Church of Christ, New York, maintains that even when a local congregation tries to change and respond to people and the times "as

---

* Wentz expresses this in an article, "Save Your Clerical Collars, Boys!", in *The Christian Century*, September 3, 1969. Mary McDermott Shideler's article, "An Ancient Word for Modern Churches," appeared in *The Christian Century* December 16, 1970. Erickson's words are from an unpublished monograph, "Prospects for a Changing Church," dated November, 1969. The Kersten quotations are from his book, *The Lutheran Ethic*, published in 1970 by Wayne State University Press, Detroit.

they really are," failure is the normal experience. The first split among the members is ideological, and the second tactical, he says, in his "review of much literature on 'renewed' churches."

Conservative, "confessional" churches are included in the struggle, according to Lawrence L. Kersten, assistant professor of sociology at Eastern Michigan University. He describes "the growing gulf" between theologically liberal Lutheran clergymen and the large majority of Lutheran laity.

Possibly the best summary of the last 10 years is Jeffrey K. Hadden's *The Gathering Storm in the Churches.** Professor of sociology and urban studies at Tulane University, New Orleans, Louisiana, Hadden maintains that the Protestant churches are in a deep crisis over *purpose* and *meaning, belief* and *authority.* In each of these, Hadden sees the laity and clergy being pulled farther and farther apart.

And none of the studies mentioned here deals directly with the local church and its young people. For at least the last decade youth have been leaving the church in droves. Adults who comforted themselves with the idea that they would return "when they're married and settled down," are now realizing that prediction no longer is true. A significant number of young people do accept and hold on to most of their parent's values and beliefs. Those who do not, however, are increasing and are more open about it.

Few churches honestly believe they have a strong hold on the young.

If all of this seems disjointed, it is. A summary or

---

* Jeffrey K. Hadden, *The Gathering Storm in the Churches.* Garden City: Doubleday, 1970.

composite of all the studies would be very difficult. There is no singular problem or dilemma. Maybe the studies themselves are part of the problem.

At the very least, the fact that such critical writings and studies have been appearing for a decade says that (a) the local church is, or has been, important and is worth bothering about; (b) if the local church has survived all this criticism, it either has some real life left in it, or is dreadfully entrenched, and perhaps both, and (c) the accumulation of criticism does point to deep-seated dissatisfaction with what is or is not going on in the local congregation.

I repeat that there is no single sore to be lanced, cauterized or removed. This clinical chart, however, seems to reveal to me that the relationship or lack of relationship between the laity and the clergy is one of the crucial aspects of the dilemma. My feeling has grown out of some two years of working in or near a couple dozen Protestant congregations. It echoes some of what Jeffrey Hadden says, but reverberates off some additional walls.

And a wall is probably the best description for what lies between laity and clergy. It's not a gap. A gap is empty. It's a wall. A wall is often solid, tall, forbidding, discouraging and not easy to surmount.

Who built the wall?

4.

IN THIS CORNER—
THE CLERGY!

For one thing, the clergy built the wall.

Clergymen are religious people; most of them are believers, and that's the way it should be.

But believing, we noted before, is tricky business. What you believe, how you believe it, and what inferences you draw from what you believe, are important but not always consistent.

Part of the church's difficulty in our society comes from what the clergy believe and don't believe—about themselves, about the church, about the world, about the members of their congregations, and about God who comes to clergymen in themselves, in the church, in the world, and in the members of the congregations.

Discussing clergymen is not the most interesting pastime in the world, even if you are one. We'll keep this chapter brief. But it's important to know about the presumed and the real hang-ups of those leaders people are counting on to help the church make it.

We have learned from surveys most of what we know about clergymen. Researchers have developed surveys that are quite reliable, as long as we recognize the limita-

17

tions of survey-making and survey-taking. The best researchers are cautious about their findings.

Our other source of information is seeing, being, knowing, watching, following, leading, talking to, listening to,
wondering, and thinking about clergymen. You can do
this as well as I. The rest of this chapter is a composite
of a number of clergymen I know, including myself. It's
not true of all clergymen, or even of any one clergyman.
In my opinion, it's fairly true of a lot of clergymen.

And it contributes to the building of the wall.

1. *The clergyman works with an "authority model" in
   his relationship with the members of his congregation.*

"So what's new?" many will ask. What else do you
expect of one who is supposed to speak for God? Most
are so accustomed to this pattern, they wouldn't give it a
second thought.

But it's worth a second thought. A clergyman is legitimately expected to be an authority on religion, theology,
the Bible, God, and the relationship of God, man, and the
world. He is a specialist, someone who has studied and
has had a certain amount of experience in a certain field.
He may well be an authority, also, on public speaking,
education, how people work together, public worship,
and so on.

In his relationship with his congregation, he also works
with an "authority model" when he looks upon his contact with members as one in which he is the answer-man
and they are the questioners.

The term "authority model" means the clergyman usually sees people as sick and himself as the healer; he sees
people always as learners and himself as teacher; he sees
people only as listeners and himself as spokesman; he sees

people as consistently in doubt, in darkness and without truth, and sees himself as confident, in the light, and dispenser of truth.

That's a hang-up.

2. *The clergyman sees himself caught in the middle of difficult and often opposing pressures.*

As the clergyman recognizes the wide range of interest, response and commitment of his members, he frequently sees himself as having to serve some members at the expense of others. He feels the risk of supporting some in a way that will offend others.

At times he finds himself modifying his beliefs, intensifying some and grasping at others in new ways. He feels caught in the dilemma of how to share these new views, feelings, and attitudes.

He often feels trapped between emphases and actions designed to get the congregation to act on what they say, and those which are geared to survival of the parish. He walks a tightrope between his concern for individuals and the effort he devotes to corporate activities. He sees himself pulled between churchly influences and worldly influences, and he struggles between the choices of quality and quantity, spiritual aliveness and statistical comparisons.

That's a hang-up.

3. *The clergyman does not know the members of his congregation as well as he thinks or claims.*

Clergymen and congregation members are mobile. Our clock-ridden society allows less and less time for knowing people well.

Besides, many churches have a tradition of keeping

distance between clergy and laity. He's not supposed to hear normal conversations, street language, bitter disagreements, serious criticism, emotional outbursts. When social contacts do occur, most of the conversation centers on the church, church activities, religious thought and carefully-screened topics.

Even in small congregations, serious, personal conversations about goals, vocations, values, issues, and commitment tend to be rare except in times of crisis. So, much of what laity and clergy know about each other is guesswork, if not prejudice.

Some clergymen as a matter of conviction, avoid friendship with the laity. They contend it hinders the "pastoral" relationship. Others avoid closeness with members to whom they genuinely respond as human beings for fear of misunderstanding among other members. And some cannot let go of their authority model long enough to be a friend.

And that's a hang-up.

4. *The clergyman increasingly distrusts the members of his congregation.*

Trust is an instinctive, unquestioning belief in and reliance on a person. A relationship of trust within a local congregation is more than simply counting on someone to show up at a meeting or to usher at a service or to make agreed-upon phone calls. Rather, it is a conscious trust built on good reasons out of past experience.

The clergyman is wary of the members of his congregation, however. He holds them at a distance and rarely comes to a trusting relationship. Like anyone else, clergymen have been burned in trusting relationships. They have experienced disappointment, suspicion, gossip, and hurt. In the complexity that is a parish, they prefer to meet and deal "objectively" with one and all. "That way," they say, "no one gets hurt."

And that way, some of us reply, "no one gets helped." Or at least, fewer people are reached in ways that are deep and lasting.

And that's a hang-up.

5. *The clergyman seldom has clear goals for the congregation or for his own ministry at this particular time.*

The local clergyman sees himself in a crisis ministry more than in a growth ministry. By training or preference, he spends more time in solving problems and dealing with crises than in building the potential of the members. The goal of growth and development is constantly affirmed but seldom consciously followed, even in a crisis.

One clergyman said he discovered that he spent most of his time unconsciously waiting for a crisis, and if none appeared, the Sunday morning experience became the crisis of the week.

Possibly the most embarrassing question a local clergyman faces is this: "What is the purpose of your congregation?" The quick answers, "preach the Word of God" and "help people," are given, but little is said about specific goals and objectives for this particular clergyman in this particular congregation at this particular time.

It may be true that trying to be all things to all men has made clergymen ministers of none. "Religion-in-general" is not the exclusive domain of the laity. Many a clergyman has nothing more specific in mind than *words,* like sin, forgiveness, faith, God, Christ, hope, life, heaven.

And *that's* a hang-up.

6. *And finally, the clergyman does not see himself as an enabler of the potential of the members of his congregation.*

Seeing himself as the authority in the congregation, the clergyman nevertheless finds himself trapped between opposing and confusing pressures. He does not know his members well, can manipulate most of them if he chooses, and increasingly sees them as "the enemy."

The members are the clients, the patients, the consumers, the followers. For personal, theological or phychological reasons, the clergyman does not believe in their potential as Christians or as human beings. He does not expect them to lead boldly, teach creatively, counsel seriously, or decide independently. They cannot support one another, much less him.

As he sees it, he is the giver rather than the receiver, the teller rather than the listener, the analyzer rather than the accepter, the director rather than the co-worker, the dispenser rather than the enabler.

And that's a hang-up.

The clergy have built the wall between themselves and the laity.

But that's not the whole story.

5.

✳✳✳✳✳✳✳✳✳✳✳✳✳✳✳✳✳✳✳✳✳✳✳✳✳✳✳✳✳✳✳✳✳

AND IN THIS CORNER—
THE LAITY!

The rest of the story is that the laity also have built the
wall between themselves and the clergy. Like the clergymen, the congregation members are not always aware
of what's happening between them. They take a lot for
granted . . . accept a lot, assume a lot and strangely,
often as not, like their lot in congregational life.

It's an important lot but it's definitely a sub-lot. Activity can be involved, or it can be non-activity. Either
way, some messages are coming through to whomever
will take the time to look and listen.

Youth are laity. They are a sub-plot of the sub-lot. Laity
in a congregation often are treated like youth; to be seen
and not heard. In recent years church young people have
been trying to break out of the back lot. Some have begun
(not too loudly) to ask questions. Some have begun to
ask for changes in worship styles and forms. Some main-
line church youth have broken away from the churches
of their childhood. Some have joined or developed non-
church, even anti-church, religious groups—hippies,
Jesus People, Spirit Movement, Eastern religions.

When they do, they're not liked by the laity in the

mainline churches. They are called radicals, malcontents, even revolutionaries. They are not accepting their seemingly-decreed-from-eternity roles of hapless followers of the clergy. They're on the other side of the wall.

And they like it that way.

Generalizations are dangerous, but important and helpful at the same time. The six observations listed here are based on findings by Jeffrey Hadden, Peter Berger, Lawrence Kersten, and others. But mostly they reflect what I have learned from and about a varied group of suburban Protestant and Catholic lay people over the years, and especially the last three years.

These generalizations are not true of all laity, to be sure, or even of any one lay person. In my opinion, they are fairly true of a lot of lay people.

And they also help build the wall.

1. *The layman limits the interest, presence and power of God to what are called "spiritual things."*

We talked about this in Chapter 2. Lay people have been taught and intensely believe that God is a spirit and that, therefore, "the things of God" are spiritual. Faith, hope, and love are compartmentalized into certain "religious," usually mental, activities.

Ordinarily, the judgment of God is seen as against everything not sponsored or approved by the church. Faithful churchgoers are seen as having exclusive claim upon the mercy of God. Christ's teachings about the kingdom of God are identified with the church. And God's concern, presence, and power among all people, nations and societies, and in all his creation, is seen as incidental if not accidental.

The local congregation is supposed to take care of

those specific "spiritual things" and to keep its nose out of everything else.

That's wall-building thinking.

2. *The layman Americanizes God and religion.*

The laity has been taught and intensely believes that God is comfortably old, very American, certainly Caucasian, terribly rich, and completely capitalistic. As Peter Berger says, Christianity is *identified* with our culture, with the way people in American think, act, and hope.

We've seen so many movies with unreal but happy, middle-class endings that most lay people believe God couldn't possibly be serious about judgment. If we let everything alone, the good guys (us) will win and the bad guys (them) will lose, as they always do in a John Wayne film.

And, therefore, God is on our side. Anyone who questions, argues, or disagrees with our ideas or teachings or way of doing things is un-godly. If we use biblical language and follow the democratic process, God won't let us down on that last day. Nor in our local congregation.

That's wall-building thinking.

3. *The layman trivializes the church.*

The laity has been taught and intensely believes that the ceremonial duties of the local congregation are crucial to the Christian faith and the survival of God. Frequently more importance and effort are given to the functions of the acolyte or the arrangements of flowers on the altar than to the quality of relationships in the congregation.

Every congregation must have a constitution, especially one with a carefully-worded clause concerning what to do with the real estate if the group should disagree or dissolve. Printed reports also seem to be considered a sign of the kingdom of God. One wag wanted to call his church, "The Christian Church of the Mimeograph!"

Current humor identifies the seven last words of the church as, "We never did it that way before." The cutting edge of the joke is not the unwillingness to change, but the preoccupation with "the way" of doing things.

That's wall-building thinking.

4. *The layman fears the social implications of the Gospel.*

This is the important reverse side of the coin mentioned under number 1 above. The laity has been taught and intensely believes that the way to distort and corrupt God, religion, and Jesus Christ is to make direct application of the Christian faith to the corporate, social, and moral problems of the day.

Concern for a Christian response to obvious, identifiable injustice, repression, violence, hunger, poverty, as well as concerns about politics, the young, the elderly, sexuality, and race are seen as a substitute for "real religion."

There is real fear involved. However, it is not always clear whether it is fear of losing the faith, fear of real life, fear of people in need, or fear of self.

In any case, that's wall-building thinking.

5. *The layman acts out of self-interest.*

The laity has been taught and intensely believes in individual piety and salvation. They have responded to the warnings about "losing *your* soul" and "accepting Christ as *your* personal Savior." And logically enough, they are convinced that anything that may interfere with the security of their own piety, salvation, or personal happiness is neither godly nor good.

The layman, therefore, has been taught to act out of his own self-interest. Any attempt to influence the laity *to act*—on the basis of doctrine, conscience, or human need—against what he thinks is his self-interest will result in much talk and no action.

The laity's commitment centers on self-interest. It will last as long as that self-interest is served, and no longer.

That's wall-building thinking.

6. *The layman makes the clergyman what he is.*

This really hurts the laity, and it seems to fly in the face of what was said in the previous chapter about the authority model of the clergy.

In spite of the authority hang-up, the clergy give the laity what they *think* the laity want. The laity do not accurately or adequately convey their wants and hopes and fears and needs to the clergy. They may not be sure themselves of what they really want, and what they want may not always be what they really need in order for the congregation to make it. Still, what the clergy *think* the laity want is what they get.

In a real sense, the laity hold the trump cards. They think the clergy are in charge. The clergy think they are giving the laity what they want.

And obviously, that's wall-building thinking.

6.

"... I CALL YOU FRIENDS"

Enough of the analysis. We affirm that the wall between laity and clergy exists. It is of varying height, depth, and width. Clergy and laity alike have built it and maintain it.

Doors are entrances or exits. They symbolize freedom for or freedom from. And in between are the walls. A room must have walls to have doorways. But life has a sense of freedom and hope when it is lived in doorways as well as within walls.

Everyone has doors to be opened. People are looking for the handles that open them to dealing more realistically with life. The church is called to help people to deal with life. The local congregation is not life itself but it may, and can, provide some handles to open doors into life—doors in the walls we and others have built around ourselves.

One sizable, attractive door is friendship. I offer it as a serious, basic response to the wall between laity and clergy. Let me tell you why. And then how I think it can work.

Recently some church researchers set out to learn what people want in an adult leader who works with youth in behalf of the church. Most young people responded that, more than competence, faith or even maturity, they wanted a person who is accepting, understanding, and alive. The adults favored competence and faith, but agreed with youth that the crucial element is acceptance.

I believe they were saying they wanted someone who could be a friend.

From another perspective, it's interesting to take a look at the relationship Jesus Christ developed with his disciples. One could argue that this was long ago and far away, or that the disciples were more than lay members of a congregation. But I think the relationship is not only applicable but actually the key to understanding Christ's ministry and message.

Christ's outlandish, unbelievable acts—we call them miracles—attracted crowds. His speech was direct and authoritative. The common people heard him gladly. The opposition soon recognized the power of his message and his following. But again and again he pointed out that he came not to be served but to serve. And St. John provides a deep insight when he records Christ's words: "I do not call you servants any longer, because a servant does not know what his master is doing. Instead, I call you friends, because I have told you everything I heard from my father" (John 15:15).

Something more was going on between Jesus and his followers than rabbinical education. Lazarus is called his "dear friend." The disciple next to him at the Last Supper is called his "beloved." Because these were male-to-male relationships, our sex-filled society raises eyebrows at this kind of writing. But personal intimacy is what Jesus had with his disciples. The greatest love a man can have for his friends is to give his life for them.

He gave his life for them, and he told them *everything* he heard from his Father. Deuteronomy describes a friend as one "who is as your own soul," one with whom you share your life.

Andrew Greeley, a Roman Catholic priest and program director for the National Opinion Research Center at the University of Chicago, has written a book called *The Friendship Game.** He gave the book the subtitle: "Reflections on the most pleasurable and the most difficult of human activities—friendship." Interestingly, he recalls that he was trained as a priest to believe that he was not permitted to have friendships. Then, he continues, he made the discovery "in middle years, after the Vatican Council, that friendship was at the very core of the Christian message."

Some of the newer translations of the Scriptures make his observation quite clear. St. Paul, in writing about becoming a new being joined to Christ, says, "All this is done by God, who through Christ changed us from enemies into his friends, and gave us the task of making others his friends also" (II Corinthians 5). According to Paul, the big message of Christians is, "Let God change you from enemies into friends!"

Simple deduction: If Christianity is about being friends with God because of Jesus Christ, why not laity and clergy in local congregations being friends because of Christ?

Will it work? Do we know what a friend is? Can you "organize" the making of friendships? Can you have a friend if you have never consciously been a friend?

The neat thing is that many people consider adolescence "the" time for friendships. Usually that means

---

* Andrew M. Greeley, *The Friendship Game.* Garden City: Doubleday, 1970.

with people of the same age. Could it possibly be that young people will lead the way in breaking down the wall between laity (themselves) and clergy (their pastor friends in a year or two. It's not easy. But once he is com-about it?

Let's take a look at what this would mean. First, the clergyman:

Undoubtedly it means that the clergyman will begin to deepen his relationships with the members he feels closest to and possibly those he sees the most. This takes time, but not nearly as much as one first thinks. It takes time for talking about things not related to church activity. It takes time to reassure each other of honest intent and sincerity.

Working at friendship is awkward, if not impossible. Being open to get to know another human being well, beyond casual and surface matters, is also awkward at first, but it is possible. And it can lead to friendship.

It is wise not to expect too much too soon. Friendship evolves slowly. It can neither be mass-produced nor created instantaneously. Friendship has to be open so that each person feels free to end the relationship. This is a threat in a local congregation because cooling a friendship with the pastor may seem to be a loss of the faith. Unless it is free, it will not be friendship.

There are many levels of friendship. The clergyman may not be able to garner more than two or three close friends in a year or two. It's not easy. But once he is committed to friendship, his outlook towards all members can change.

In his book, *The Ways of Friendship,** Ignace Lepp, a Roman Catholic priest and a practicing psychotherapist

---

* Ignace Lepp, *The Ways of Friendship.* New York: Macmillan, 1968.

in Paris before his death, argues that anyone who has known one real friendship will benefit from it in all his relationships. For the local congregation, this would indicate that even a few friendships would improve the clergyman's relationship with the laity.

And what does friendship with the clergyman mean for the laity?

For one thing it means relating to someone who accepts you as *you* are, virtues, faults, needs, and all. It means being part of a relationship that is not blind to faults but one in which both persons see more deeply, beyond the externals of looks, speech, posture, and habits, and beyond the unconscious motivations for so much of what we do. Most human beings crave such acceptance.

Laity and clergy share in the loneliness and anxiety of the age. Friendship is an antidote. There is someone to phone, to talk to, to remember, someone who knows and cares. Perhaps the essence of friendship is to reassure another person that she or he need not be afraid of us. Andrew Greeley* warns that this is a difficult message to get across. "Most of us are shocked to learn that we terrify others even though we are all too painfully aware that others terrify us." We think we have a monopoly on terror. Friendship is an invitation to put aside terror.

Friendship means equality. It reaches beyond age. Ever see a 2-year-old playing with her 75-year-old grandmother? It reaches beyond intellect to include spirit, feelings, and heart.

Friendship cannot survive when one person dominates or obligates another. Each must be free to bring

---

* In *The Friendship Game,* page 26.

what each has to the relationship. We are drawn to those most like us in attitudes, values, and backgrounds and to those we feel accept and want us. But mutuality is essential for friendship. We really cannot carry or be carried by a friend for long.

Friendship suggests allowing ourselves to be trusted and known. It implies sticking with each other even at a cost to ourselves. It is built on care and love freely demonstrated in both directions. Friendship doesn't see the barriers that keep us from one another. It can happen between truck drivers and college professors, custodians and bank presidents, career girls and homemakers, young and old, black and white, liberals and conservatives, laity and clergy.

There is risk involved in friendship. This is especially true of friendships between men and women. There is a close bond between our emotions and our sexual impulses. There is a risk of misunderstanding oneself and each other. There is a risk of being misunderstood by others.

There is risk involved because one can lose at the friendship game. To be rejected is most difficult.

There is risk involved because of the importance of hanging on to our own integrity while we give ourselves to another in friendship. That is not easy, either.

And if adolescence *is* the time for friendships, youth may well have a dominant role to play in making changes in local congregations. It can happen between the young and the clergy. It can happen among the young themselves, and with parents and with other adults.

Friendship has the greatest potential for sharing of any evangelism plan. The goal is not to capture or manipulate but to build a trusting and open relationship. It can happen between peers. It can happen with teachers at school. It can even happen with sisters and brothers.

Freedom and friendship can go hand-in-hand. Friendship can mean helping another person find a door where once he saw only a wall.

The urge to be ourselves for one another is a powerful human urge. Coupled with the liberating Gospel of Jesus Christ, it is powerful enough to break down the wall between laity and clergy.

7.

✶✶✶✶✶✶✶✶✶✶✶✶✶✶✶✶✶✶✶✶✶✶✶✶✶✶✶✶✶✶✶✶✶✶✶✶

HUMAN BEINGS OF GOD

Originally, the title of this chapter was "The People of God." But somehow that didn't quite say it. I hope the revised title will help get these ideas across more directly.

What's-in-a-name is an old question. What we call another person or ourselves can make a difference. It may even reveal serious thoughts and feelings about others or ourselves. For instance, we have grouped people as laity and clergy. All of them are human beings, but it was easier to talk about them by labeling them. It would have been far more difficult to say what we said if we had just called them people or human beings. So, labels make a difference.

Churches label people. People who do not belong to their group are called non-members, unchurched, prospects, or even pagans, or "the world."

And for those who are members there is a hierarchy of labels: baptised members, communicant members, confirmed members, delinquent members, associate members, voting members, and, probably on the top of the heap, contributing members.

All of these members, including delinquents, are people. And in the best Christian circles, all of them could well be called "the people of God." The term "laity" really means "people." And in church teaching, "the people" are "the people of God."

That's better than names like associate members, communicant members, and contributing members. But I think "human beings of God" is even better, although I don't like the way it sounds and I don't think masses of people will start using it. Human beings are what God and the church are all about, but, as we have seen, human beings are not what the local congregation is all about. The congregation *believes* it is all about God but that's only true in a sense. If the local congregation takes God seriously, it has to be *primarily* about human beings.

Here's how one human being of God, Louis Evely, a Roman Catholic priest and author says it: "Christ is the Copernicus of religion: before him everything revolved around the worship of God—how to appease God, how to find favor with him, how to calm our fears by giving him his ration of honors, gold and blood. Christ made everything revolve around the service of man. True worship of God is respect for man."*

Evely goes on to point out that to pagans, all kinds of things are sacred: monkeys, cows, buildings, altars, woods, mountains. Everything, that is, except man. "But for Christ, man alone is sacred, and everything else is at his service—*even God!*"

One more sentence from Evely: "God shows himself through you if God in you loves your brothers much better than if God in you loves himself."

In other words, God is about human beings, and for human beings, and in human beings, and with human beings. That's the entire meaning of God. Think about it.

---

* Louis Evely, *Our Prayer.* New York: Herder and Herder, 1970.

So if the local congregation is going to make it, its chief priority must be human beings. It has to make its reputation inside the congregation, in the neighborhood, the community, the nation, and society as being about and for and in and with human beings.

Two obstacles: Too many people still believe that God is about himself. They think, for instance, that the biblical descriptions of God are ends in themselves—for instance, that he is all-powerful, all-knowing, all-present, everywhere, as though he tells us about himself to scare us or show off. Those descriptions are *in behalf of* human beings. God is all-powerful so human beings can depend on the power he makes available—physical, spiritual, intellectual, cosmic, emotional. God reveals himself as all-knowing so human beings can count on things not getting totally out of hand. We're tied to day-by-day, if not minute-by-minute events and decisions. But Someone knows and Someone cares.

The grace of God exists for human beings. The judgment of God is loosed so that human beings will catch on to it and not wreck themselves and others. The creation of God, earth, sky, sea, planets, is given into the all-too-fumbling hands of human beings. The love of God is for human beings. God loved human beings so much that he gave his only Son, so that every human being who believes in him may not die but have eternal life.

Now that's being for human beings!

The other obstacle to local congregations being *for* human beings is that some human beings aren't very human. They seem less than human-like, sub-human, anti-human, animal, even demonic. Scriptures call this "sin," this making of yourself an enemy of God and, therefore, of man. But it's a fact—most human beings are not very human. They're distorted.

And local congregations, like many of us, become angry and upset with distorted human beings. We almost think we're God. God was upset with distorted humanity, too, but he did something about it. He corrected the distortion through the fully and authentically human birth, life, death, and resurrection of his Son. And Christians believe that God, because of his Son, is still very, very sold on human beings, even those distorted beings inside or outside the church.

God loves human beings. He sent his Son to be one.

The aim of the local congregation can be to work for the full humanity which God intends for his creation, particularly for man and his society. Philip Hefner, professor of systematic theology at the Lutheran School of Theology, Chicago, thinks the church ought to regain its understanding of itself "as the guardian of the humanity which the world seeks."* Christians believe this was made clear by Jesus Christ, the most perfect example of humanity.

Psychology and psychotherapy would describe "authentically human" as being *fully born*, to develop one's awareness, one's reason, one's capacity for life" in a way that goes beyond selfishness and ties us into real unity with the world.

Christianity adds the value of a God-loved human being, called into unity with God himself, with all that is good and lasting and worthwhile, and sent to live joyfully and usefully in a world made for human beings.

Sounds like God's out and man's in? Not really. Rather, it's a determination to put together again the great commandments of love which so often are torn apart: love God with heart, soul, mind, love your fellow human be-

---

* From an unpublished address, "Theological Perspectives on Social Ministry," 1969.

ing as yourself. There's a huge "AND" implied between those two phrases. They're connected. The first is greatest but the second is "like it." Love of God is expressed in loving human beings with God's own love.

Sound like heaven's out and earth is in? Not really. Rather, it's a determination to live God's life now, rather than to wait for death. His life lasts right on through death. That's really living, and it begins in the local congregation with human beings called laity and clergy. They are alive and they think and feel and wonder and fail and discover and grow and hope and fantasize and doubt and believe.

There are in it,—life,—together because of God. They are human beings of God.

8.

✗✗✗✗✗✗✗✗✗✗✗✗✗✗✗✗✗✗✗✗✗✗✗✗✗✗✗✗✗✗✗✗✗✗✗✗

EARTH IS NOT
A DESERT DREAR

Human beings live on earth.

That's the best information we have as of this writing. We've had human beings spinning around the earth and walking on the moon, but a major goal of those space probes was to get the human beings back to earth again.

The local congregation is located on earth where the human beings it's made up of live. Among many other things, they are citizens of this planet.

The local congregation's attitude toward where it finds itself situated is one of the obstacles to the congregation's making it. In various ways, the congregation seems to say that it would far rather be in heaven than on earth.

That sounds like a legitimate objective. Christians believe life goes on after death. But the local congregation does not go on. It's stuck with this planet, which really is not bad, once you think it through. And once you stop singing some questionable 19th century hymns, like "I'm But a Stranger Here, Heav'n is my Home," and especially its notorious second line, "Earth is a desert drear, Heav'n is my home."

Christians legitimately consider themselves "citizens

of heaven," as St. Paul suggests in Philippians 3. It does not follow, however, that we must hate where we are now. God created earth and heaven. Christ redeemed "all things in heaven and on earth." So to be sold on heaven as God's eventual, eternal gift does not automatically mean being anti-earth.

Especially for the members of an earth-bound organization like the local congregation.

The hang-up, if you'll hang on during this side trip, come from the many words and meanings the Bible uses for "the world." Sometimes the biblical words point to time more than to space, such as "world without end," and "the world to come." But even the word used most frequently in the New Testament for "spatial world" has at least five meanings going for it in different places. It can refer to the universe as a whole or to the planet earth; to people in general, or to the scene of human activity; to the fallen race of mankind at enmity with God, or to the scene and object of God's redeeming action.

No wonder we're not clear. We have a right to be at odds with "the world" when it means opposition to what God does and wants. But certainly we should not be against "the world" as the place where God is continuously carrying out his salvation among men. Jesus is the Lamb of God removing the sins of the world. He is the Light of the world. God was in him reconciling the world to himself.

If the local congregation wants to make it, for God and with his human beings in his world, it has to stop viewing the world as an ecclesiastical no-man's land. Jesus Christ is the Lord of the world, even of that part of the world that rejects him and fights the will and way of his Father.

Out there in the world of human activity is where "it"

really happens, for the local congregation. Or does not happen. Christ prays to his Father for his disciples because, "I sent them into the world just as you sent me into the world." And again, "Just as I do not belong to the world, they do not belong to the world." But, he adds, "I do not ask you to take them out of the world but I do ask you to keep them safe from the Evil One."

In the world, all the way; but not of the world, no way. A tough and tricky assignment for human beings of God gathered in a local congregation.

When we feel an eagerness to get this life over with and pick up our crown in heaven—sometimes because we're tired of the drag, sometimes because we're really sold on the promises of God, and sometimes because we're just plain scared of what's going on in the world— heaven and the congregation seem much, much safer.

But like Christ, we are sent to the world, and we ought accept and know the world as our place to be and live and work and hope. That's not easy. Jacques Ellul, a layman of the French Reformed Church and professor of law and government at the University of Bordeaux, claims we are caught between two necessities, which nothing can alter: ". . . on the one hand it is impossible for us to accept it as it is."* According to Ellul, accepting this tension in life, not just in theory, is the avenue leading toward learning how the Christian faith can speak to the modern pagan of our world.

He goes on: "In reality, today the theologian has nothing to say to the world, because there are no 'laymen' in our churches . . ." By this he means the clergy do not know the situation in the world because of their restricted roles and activities. And the laymen escape from

---

* Jacques Ellul, *The Presence of the Kingdom*. New York: Seabury Press, 1967.

the world by keeping their faith and their life in the world in different compartments.

The Holy Spirit has bridged bigger gaps than this before, but throughout the course of history, most of the time God has used material means to accomplish his objectives. In other words, God acts by his Spirit through human instruments: people, human beings of God, the laymen. They are the point of contact with the world.

When the church views the world only as a desert drear, or as strictly enemy territory, the laity fails to see its task and opportunity in the world. And they simply work hard building up antagonism for "the world" out there, while congregations get them to do more and more clergy-type things back at the religion place, the local congregation.

We're looking once again at the individual piety versus the social concern dilemma. The person, as human being, is basic. The local church cannot make it if it does not make it with human beings. That means helping persons to be as fully human as they are able to be through the renewing power of the love of God, made known in Jesus Christ.

Treating God as a doctrine and people simply as doctrine receivers, readers, understanders, and discussers is anti-biblical and anti-personal. God reveals himself in relationship to mankind and in relationships among human beings of God.

All of being human counts in this relationship: thinking, feeling, wanting, touching, seeing, speaking, smelling, tasting (don't forget the Sacrament), and everything else that goes into the receiving and giving processes of human beings.

The current craving for personal, even intimate, relationships with other human beings ought to find at least part of its fulfillment among people who have been turned on to redeemed humanity in Jesus Christ. The church is for the personalness of human beings.

But turned-on persons live in society, in the world, the scene of human activities. We belong to each other, not only in terms of closeness and affection but in terms of our oneness with all men. Many church people have been so busy warning about the watering down of brotherhood that they have come close to denying the brotherhood of all mankind. Many people have spent so much time identifying the uniqueness of individuals and groups that they have been in danger of losing sight of the great commonalities we all share as human beings.

Besides, the globe is a tight fit now. Everywhere is only hours away, and seconds by radio or television. We are our brother's keepers. "From the one man God created all races of men, and made them live over the whole earth."

How we relate to one another in the local congregation is an important demonstration of what is happening to each of us personally. How the local congregation relates to the world around it, to the people of the neighborhood, the community, the state, and the nation is an equally important, and sometimes a more critical test of what is happening in each of us personally.

How groups of congregations, banded together in councils or denominations, relate to the part of the world that does not acknowledge God or his Son is a further demonstration of what is happening through each of us personally.

Jesus was decisive on this point: "You are salt for all mankind." You are to be tasted and savored by others. There's no sense in simply keeping salt on a shelf.

"You are like light for the whole world," he said. How foolish to hide that light under a barrel. No one will be able to see. "Your light must shine before people, so that they will see the good things you do and give praise to your Father in heaven."

Salt gets lost in the soup. You don't say the salt is souped. No, the soup is salted—all of it, not selectively so that part is salted and other parts are not. If salt gets into the soup, the soup is salted.

Light moves out into the entire room. You don't say the light is roomed. No, the room is lighted—all of it, not selectively so that part is lighted and other parts are not. If the light is turned on in the room, the room is lighted.

Selectivity and exclusiveness are man's problems. God is inclusive. All creation, all people, all human activity are his and his creation and his people and his activity.

The world is no desert drear, no ecclesiastical no-man's land. The world is the arena of the life of love of God's human beings.

9.

✗✗✗✗✗✗✗✗✗✗✗✗✗✗✗✗✗✗✗✗✗✗✗✗✗✗✗✗✗✗✗✗✗✗✗✗

FRANKLY,
THE ODDS ARE BAD . . .

That's the honest truth. The odds are bad, on the basis of what we know and what we can guess, for the local congregation making it in the sense we have been talking about.

This does not mean local congregations are going to curl up and die, or burn themselves down, or even disappear in the immediate future.

The local church is in trouble, but it is not gone. It may remain and stay in trouble. It may eventually fade from the scene. It may slowly accept some serious, even drastic changes and make it once again. But the odds are bad.

Some people say the local gathering of Christians never really has made it in the sense we're talking about. That it is the nature of the congregation always to be in process—to be hanging on to what it was, struggling with what it is and, beyond that, what it could be. But it's hard to find authorization from either God or man for this thinking. The local church often is all too open to failure. Because of forgiveness, some are quick to say, we can't afford to fail.

Is it less true or less Christian to say that, because of forgiveness, the local church can afford to succeed? Sometimes, it seems, Christians are almost afraid to do something that pleases God and serves the needs of man.

People have tried. A variety of experiments in change and renewal are on record. Interestingly, most of them are not centered in local congregations. Most efforts, by far, have been in the "special ministries" where there have been a whole spate of experiments, outside a local congregation or with only faint ties to it. Local and area denominational leaders and/or interchurch groups have sponsored special ministries to dwellers in high-rise apartments and young adult apartment complexes, to motorcycle gangs, to racetrack workers, to airline personnel. There is a variety of chaplaincy programs on campuses, in hospitals, in factories, among the military, in shopping centers and metropolitan night life areas, and in the entertainment field generally.

A 1969 study of new forms of ministry by the Department of Church Renewal of the National Council of Churches of Christ in the U.S.A. indicated that "nearly eight out of ten of the new forms report performing types of services not generally associated with the program of the local church." The highest number of projects involved ecumenical efforts which helped the church minister to people with special needs.

This does not mean that local congregations could not sponsor or participate in such ministries. All it says is that in these efforts, they did not. There are classic exceptions. Some congregations, scattered across the United States, have seriously tried to change their goals and their style of life. Their rarity highlights the findings given above.

Some experiments at renewal were closer to the local

congregational scene. The "house" church, for instance, has been tried as a sort of half-way structure between the church and the world. Supported by the existing congregation, the house church offers an opportunity for small groups of Christians, often families, to join together, to worship and to reflect, to plan and to act together as a smaller cadre of believers. Strict formality and complex structures are by-passed. People seem to feel wanted, needed, and involved.

Prominent in England for some years, the house church has not caught on in the United States as widely as predicted four or five years ago.

The underground church seems to have lost its spark and influence, except in very small circles. There is no doubt about its impact on the traditional churches. Many new forms of worship now found even in staid local congregations were inspired by, if not directly developed, in underground congregations. Many such groups continue to serve special, important needs. Wisely or not, many consider them a cop-out, contending that almost anything can be tried if the opposition is first carefully sifted out.

Business-Industrial Missions also have made an impact upon local congregations in some places. These missions began in Europe and are experiments in helping men and women in business and industry draw upon the Christian faith as they make the decisions, face the problems, and grasp the opportunities offered daily in their offices, factories and shops. Some local congregations have supported these efforts in their own parishes and through metropolitan, interchurch groups.

More recently local church "clusters" have been in the forefront of church renewal efforts. Clustering is designed to bring about new and varied relationships, goals, and structures among churches, persons, and community organizations. The aim is to change the life of the church. No conclusive evidence is in on the long-term value of these efforts for local congregations. At least one United Church of Christ study of cluster development tried to answer the question: "Can the local congregation be an effective resource for the ministry of the laity?" The report cites some positive results but lists more indications "pointing to a negative conclusion."

Young people have played an important role in the efforts of congregations at change and renewal. Statistics are not available, but the percentage of congregations "finally trying to do something" because they are losing their young people is very large indeed. Someone has even worked out a formula for figuring "an index of youthful vigor" for congregations and denominations. They discovered that church groups originating in the United States and having fundamentalist or pentecostal theologies tend to have a much higher percentage of young people than main-line Protestant churches.

The impact of youth in most denominations has been in group worship. Young people stopped coming to dull and dreary services where mood, music, and word seem determined to deaden if not destroy spiritual interest or ardor. The age of the guitar, of folk worship, of hymns for now, and of contemporary language is upon us. Some congregations conduct such services on a regular basis.

The results have been good in terms of attendance. Most so-called "youth services" bring a whopping increase in the number of worshipers. And a significant portion of the increase is made up of adults, including the over-60 crowd. But most changes in worship are temporizing. The old is kept with the new, and no one really expects changes to take place outside of the gathered worshipers. Making it in the worlds where the young and old handle their day-to-day decisions does not follow automatically from new forms of Sunday worship experiences.

Local congregations also have made changes in their ministries among younger members. No church is able to hold a large number of young people past junior high school age without substantial revision of approach and methods. Sunday-school-style efforts no longer work with high school students. Regeneration has a double meaning among the young people of the church. It means youth being turned on to God and it means a congregation being turned on to the new generation.

So stuffy, highly programmed youth meetings have been replaced with leadership training, coffee houses, work camps, encounter groups, hunger hikes, exchange visits between city and suburbs, traveling singers, traveling workers, traveling observers.

Slowly the local church is changing the image of its ministry to young people. For years the young had been satisfied with second-class membership in the congregation. Now, in places, young people are given opportunities to involve themselves in the life of the congregation. Increasingly, decision-making groups include youth. More adults are beginning to feel a partnership with, rather than a paternalism toward the young.

Social concerns have become a large part of the change. Some young people have been saying they want to do something about the faith of their fathers. They are children of change, a television generation that knows violence, injustice, poverty, racial unrest, and political chicanery as has no age group before them.

Protesters and hippies found little solace or success in

demonstrations. Most already had given up on the institutional church. Eastern religions were too deep and unorthodox for many. Heroes were being assassinated. The age obviously needed renewal.

The answer had to be a superstar. Thus, the Jesus people—who have thrown a scare and a delight into many local congregations. Although they are against the institutional church, they nevertheless continue to hang around local churches and local church people. Their durability and impact have not been adequately measured, but their influence, even on unsuspecting congregations, cannot be denied.

Can turned-on youth, sophisticated Bible study programs, cassette-taped evangelism campaigns, and high-powered stewardship plans accomplish what previous efforts at renewal have failed to do?

No one knows for sure. People are trying. But the odds are bad.

10.

✶✶✶✶✶✶✶✶✶✶✶✶✶✶✶✶✶✶✶✶✶✶✶✶✶✶✶✶✶✶✶✶✶✶

COMPROMISE IS NOT
A FOUR-LETTER WORD

One of the blessings local congregations miss by not knowing their laity well is the art of compromise. In one form or another, compromise is the life style of most people, including the church and its professionals, although they are reluctant to admit it.

Compromise is not a four-letter word. If you ask someone point-blank what she or he thinks of "compromise," the response is almost consistently negative. We have much more difficulty talking compromise than we do living it.

The dictionary's first definition of compromise is, "settlement of differences by mutual concessions." That's not so terrible. In fact, "mutual" and "settlement" sound almost like church words. Compromise refers to agreement reached on opposing views or by opposing forces through mutual adjustment of demands. One side gives a little; the other side gives a little. The process calls for willingness to give and ability to recognize what's worth giving and what's worth getting.

Compromise is akin to negotiation, and to words like "exchange," "interchange," "balance," and "dialogue."

And it occurs readily and frequently in daily life.

Parents set rules or goals or guidelines for their children. And often quickly compromise when the scene changes or more information becomes available.

Compromise is a workhorse in business negotiations. Adjusting one's demands and requirements for the good of all is simply daily practice. Labor-management negotiations are predicated on the desirability and usefulness of compromise. Compromise is the courage to change one's mind when more of the facts are known.

The opposite of compromise is not integrity. Only the *tenth* of the dictionary's definitions of compromise implies dishonorable or shameful concessions. The opposite of compromise is more accurately stubbornness, contention, and controversy.

The Scriptures do not picture God as being above compromise in this sense. Abraham negotiates with the Lord until the Lord promises to spare Sodom if 10 good men can be found in the city. Jacob struggles with the Lord until he extracts a blessing from him. Jesus compares a person who prays to God to a woman who simply won't stop bothering an official until he gives in and listens to her.

Possibly the grace of God itself is a form of compromise. God is just and promises to punish those who rebel, who reject him, and who thus bring about their own undoing. But God negotiates a settlement with himself; he modifies his demands, lifts the death sentence from the guilty, and places the blame and punishment upon his own Son.

Grace is God's act of self-limitation, because of his commitment to the well-being of his creatures and his creation. Compromise is by no means a four-letter word.

This may seem the long way around to suggesting that

the local congregation ought to consider compromise as its life style. In its efforts to speak for God and to proclaim his rule among men, the church often is tricked into sounding absolute. The church is not absolute; God is. The church is people . . . finite beings . . . people who make up their minds, change them, then make them up again.

Very few things the church says or does are really absolute. The church often acts as if everything it says, does, plans, or hopes is absolute. And many consider it dangerous to question or change or adapt or throw out its non-absolute ideas, formulas, or plans made by human beings.

It's not dangerous; it's desirable and necessary.

For instance, the way churches are organized, the kinds of buildings they gather in, the patterns they follow in worship, the plans they use in encouraging contributions, the language they use in teaching and preaching, the issues they choose to speak on and those they choose not to speak on . . . all these and many more are not absolutes. These decisions, choices, and preferences are subject to compromise, negotiation, adjustment, the good old give-and-take.

Compromise frees the church to respond to the self-interest of people inside and outside its membership. St. Paul was busy becoming "all things to all men" to win some of them by whatever means was possible. Our Lord was geared to the ordinary follower. The common people heard him gladly. It was worth their while.

Compromise as a life style for the local congregation takes the leadership off the hook. It commits the congregation to meet people as they are and where they are. Clergy are free to let the laity be free to speak, suggest, think, plan, and decide what the interests, concerns, and services of the local congregation ought to be. There can be less manipulation on all sides: clergy no longer compelled to "get the people into the program," and laity no longer forced to pretend they are interested when they are not. There will be little trouble hanging on to the real absolutes—love for God and love for neighbor —and to the opposites—minimizing God and people. God's will is geared to our self-interest.

Guided by these principles and open to compromise wherever necessary, the fields are ready for the harvest. Echelons of people, untouched before, can now be reached.

For instance, most churches in the United States are middle-class, made up in large part of white working people. Studies of these middle-class people are important and helpful. Their concerns ought to be at least part of the concerns of the local congregation. They are exercised about "law and order." What does the church have to say, what can it do about that? Middle-class white people are concerned about tax reform, adequate public education, occupational mobility, personal growth and mental health and high medical costs.

These are not incidentals. They are the fabric of existence for this large segment of citizens. Can the local church respond, as a church, to these issues and concerns? Can the congregation help search for accurate information, help people organize to express their opinions, to affirm or object, to gain what is legally theirs in a democratic society?

Clearly, the Gospel is also about the quality of man's life on earth. Seeking the kingdom, Jesus assures us, is not unrelated to food and shelter, job and health, family and friends. God is in charge. Jesus Christ is Lord.

Responding to the real needs, interests, and potential

of people calls for increased, legitimate involvement of the local congregation with political processes. In our land today, people are political, whether they want to be or not. Without abandoning the judgment and mercy of God and his call to share the Gospel and all that he has taught, can the local congregation seriously respond to the political processes which shape and control so much of human existence today?

Can the local church make it with modern man if it continues to refuse to do so?

Young people have a critical interest in the honesty of compromise as a way of life. The world is presently run by adults who grew up in an age momentously different from the one in which we now live. The bridge from that age to this age was built with compromises.

This is risky business. People will fear. Compromise can be a threat to what is stable within us as well as outside of us. Easy roads and safely-mapped routes will be gone. People of God will be responsible for saying where they are and listening to where others are. Together they can choose where, when, and how to begin. People may start doing all kinds of things they've never done before. Good and bad. And perhaps the human beings of God will learn again to trust in God and to count on man.

We probably won't know until we try.

11.

✶✶✶✶✶✶✶✶✶✶✶✶✶✶✶✶✶✶✶✶✶✶✶✶✶✶✶✶✶✶✶✶✶✶✶✶

SMALL IS BEAUTIFUL

Another hint for the local congregation that wants to make it: small is beautiful. This is not an easy choice in a society committed to gargantuan, larger-than-ever products and projects. For many Americans, only big is beautiful.

There are some advantages in sizeable groupings of people. Certain things can be accomplished by numbers and the power the numbers of people represent.

But small is also beautiful. And this may be an important lesson for the church in this day. At the final day, the big count will be made; the word will have gone out to the ends of the earth. But for all we know, we may be closer to the beginning than to the end of this world. Or maybe we're in the middle of God's plan for his planet.

So small still works and small still counts, as our Lord so indicated in his story about the kingdom starting like a tiny seed. Or when he said that he is present when two or three are gathered together in his name. Or when he said that the very hairs on your head counted. That's small. That's beautiful.

But the local church is having a rough time shaking the statistical syndrome. We judge a parish, a pastor, a denomination, a religion, sometimes God, himself, by the numbers game. The only one who does not publish statistics, it has been said, is the devil. He's too smart.

But God doesn't play by our rules. He isn't limited to our thought-patterns. For him a day can be a year, a year a millenium, a mite a fortune, a barn full of possessions a nothing. His spunky follower, Paul of Tarsus, had to learn that lesson. His thorn in the side, whatever it was, bothered him. Surely God would respond and rid him of it. Why, "the work of the Lord" was being hindered by his finky thorn! So Paul thought.

But the Lord cut him down to size, in love. His answer: Paul, my friend, "my grace is all you need: for my power is strongest when you are weak."

This is not a failure motif. It wasn't a particular blessing, either, to have that problem. The important thing was for Paul to learn that the love of God is stronger and more obvious where there is human need and dependence.

Is this the message the local church can learn today, that human beings who know and need God can depend upon one another in struggling to live out the will of God in an overwhelming world? But it is a world, also, in which Jesus is in charge.

Possibly, with this message learned, the congregation can be a place of acceptance and support for fellow strugglers. The congregation can be first and foremost a support group for searchers, wanderers, hopers and tryers.

A local congregation can be a very good thing. People there can take human beings seriously. People there can meet and know and love one another. There can be continuity of experience in the face of chopped-up pieces of time and life. People can interact with one another without fear—agree, disagree, question, change, rechange, interchange—and not be docked for wages or time lost or effort spent.

Theodore Erickson, in his unpublished monograph, highlights the four major aspects of the local congregational scene as, (1) Its tradition—its history and teachings, inherited from its forefathers, which usually form its purpose and self-image. (2) Its physical neighborhood—how it looks and how those who live there feel about it is related to the kind of physical property the congregation has. (3) Its community—the social, cultural, and economic circumstances of the area residents affect the members the congregation has. (4) Its mission—the activity of the congregation in the community, the things it does that extend beyond its walls, influence the program and planning of the congregation.

An examination of a parish in these terms could easily cause disappointment, and result in rash decisions to become involved with everything and anything. It is possible to over-identify with social movements. Large numbers of local congregations surely have not done so, but it is possible.

Perhaps the way to begin is for the local congregation to see itself as the place where people come when they have no other place to go. If the congregation's members, its clergy, its activities, even its buildings come to be known for acceptance, understanding and something beyond death that we call life, people well may come.

Our age keeps producing, almost in assembly-line fashion, a ragtag army of remnants: alcoholics, unmarried pregnant girls, school drop-outs, runaways. There are widows with no one to talk to. The aged are lonelier, even with television. Many people are physically, emotionally, mentally, and spiritually exhausted.

And even with Blue Cross/Blue Shield, they have no place to lay their heads.

Are the Inns of our Bethlehems still so crowded, still so busy with census-taking, that there will be no room for our neighbors in need? In the story Jesus told, the traffic on that Jericho road was constant but preoccupied. The busy travelers did not see or could not see or would not see the stranger in the ditch.

There are strangers lying all over the place today. They are rich and poor, highly educated and non-educated, old and young, white or colorfully non-white. Unattractive but beautiful because of the heavenly revelation that we meet Jesus Christ when we meet our brother in need. "Whenever," Jesus said, "you did something for one of the least important of these brothers of mine, you did it for me."

Two specific applications: the first, young people are often a powerless minority far down on our society totem pole. We neglect them at their and our own peril. It is to our interest and their interest that they be freed from the hindrances to growing to their fullest human potential. The local church can know its youth and accept them as the redeemed of God. The congregation can provide a significant home base for their growth and ministry.

Young people have much to offer. They need much. They seem small compared to some others with less economic power. But in this case again, small is beautiful and important.

The second: the non-white people of our country and the world, especially the blacks, are the most serious challenge to the honesty and aliveness of local congregations. Anyone today who does not know the truth about racism in America has chosen to be ignorant. Attitudes, actions and institutional structures combine to subordinate individuals and groups because of their color. Everyone knows it is going on. Everyone knows it is evil. Education and discussion are no longer the crucial need. Action is the only answer, action that acknowledges our failures as local churches, action that helps black people reach their fullest human potential, action that loves, accepts and supports our black sisters and brothers as we have been accepted by our Brother, Jesus Christ.

Minorities *are* small, in numbers, power, and influence. They are not always seen, much less heard. They are not more important than majorities. But they are important because God loves them and because Jesus Christ had an irritatingly consistent way of being known for associating with minorities, outcasts, and down-and-outers, without a lot of questions of how they got that way.

The voice of minorities in our society is the still, small voice of God today, saying once again that small is beautiful.

12.

✶✶✶✶✶✶✶✶✶✶✶✶✶✶✶✶✶✶✶✶✶✶✶✶✶✶✶✶✶✶✶✶✶✶✶✶

TRUSTWORTHY
RATHER THAN PREDICTABLE

The local church seems eternally adolescent. It is immature, not sure of itself or of others. It makes up its mind a dozen times and more about what it wants to become.

The local congregation, no matter how old or how big, is always becoming.

This is good. But, we have been saying, it makes a lot of difference *what* the church is becoming. As in adolescence, there are concrete choices, and the day-by-day decisions add up to important directions.

Albert van den Heuvel, director of communications for the World Council of Churches at Geneva, has written that the problem of human adolescence always has been adulthood, that is, of becoming an adult. If there is in an individual or in a society, confusion and a lack of clarity concerning what it means to be an adult, adolescence is in for a real struggle. If there is clear understanding of what adulthood is, at least an adolescent knows where he is going and can check and measure himself enroute.

Little has been done about describing the adult for our age, van den Heuvel goes on. He predicts that he will live on the road rather than in a house, will think inductively rather than deductively. His commitments will be short-term with a definite goal, his discipline will be strict, his judgments will come slowly.

More important, "the dominant traits of his character will be flexibility rather than stability, *trustworthiness rather than predictability*, curiosity rather than knowledge, an experimental attitude rather than certainty, meditation rather than preaching, listening rather than proclaiming."*

That's a favorite quote of mine, especially the phrase, "trustworthiness rather than predictability." How's that for a goal for the local congregation still in adolescence? We can put all other goals on the second shelf: warm, large, helpful, relevant, exciting, creative. What people are looking for is trustworthiness.

Like God, who is trustworthy.

With an "adult" God who is trustworthy, the local congregation can afford to be adolescent, enroute to what it is to become. And part of a wholesome adolescence is flexibility, the gift of moving back and forth, of responding to what is going on without being pushed about by every fad and whim.

With a trustworthy God, the local congregation is free to frame and reframe its own statement of purpose and functions. One congregation has done so, tossing aside traditional patterns and verbiage:

> "As members of this congregation, we will support one another to speak and act in such ways that we demonstrate publicly that the Kingdom of God is also on earth and that our daily

---

* Albert H. van den Heuvel, "A Short and Critical History of Youth Work." From *The New Creation and the New Generation*, Albert H. van den Heuvel (ed.). New York: Friendship Press, 1965.

> life is the arena where we are to minister
> among men in the name of Christ our Savior."

With a trustworthy God, the local congregation can take seriously the position of the professional ministry. The clergy's role is special. She or he is called to speak for God when others are silent or don't know what to say. Courage to be as well as to speak, discerning between comfort and challenge, between prophetic and pastoral roles, demands highly professional skill and deep personal commitment.

With a trustworthy God, the local congregation can face up to the Holy Spirit's presence in Christian teaching and living. One temptation is to forget or at least to discount the power, reality, work, and surprise of the Spirit of God, as if the Spirit were the private domain of the Pentecostals. Or a theological antique. The other temptation is to count so much on the Spirit of God that we discount or ignore the human beings of God who are the means through which the Spirit of God has chosen to be known and seen and heard. The Spirit is cool. The Spirit is aware. When we're so uptight that we don't even know *how* to pray, much less what to say, "the Spirit himself pleads with God for us . . ."

The Spirit is aware and promises to make us aware of God, of our fellowman, of the history and processes of human existence, of the trustworthiness of God, of the potential of man.

The Spirit is aware and promises to make us aware of our own selves, as individuals, and as local congregations, and of our feelings, desires, fears, ambitions, faith and hope.

With a trustworthy God, the local congregation can cry, "Hope, hope!" when there seems to be no hope. And with equal boldness announce there is no hope for that which is hopeless in the world and in the congregation.

Unlike a mindless kite, a person can choose his anchor. Not choosing an anchor means having no anchor. Having no anchor means relinquishing control and being the servant of pressures and currents. One choice of anchor is Christ.

The local church is called to make it possible for a person to grow in his attachment to Christ, to test and to soar on out and up in life with confidence. One aspect of ministry, of making it with today's people in today's world, is opening that option to people and providing for their growth.

Unless mankind is able to build a community that makes sense, man is doomed by his own willful refusal to love. Christ has offered around himself a community that makes sense. The local church is called to make it possible for a person to risk love, belong to a family, have a home. Another aspect of ministry is the growth of individuals and the entire community in their life together.

Until a person has work to do, a contribution to make to his human family, he has no reason for being and he knows it. Not being, not having meaning, is the unendurable experience. The local church holds to that Word of God that defines being/meaning/existence in terms of creativity/productivity/purpose, in terms of being involved with people to bring about mutual growth to our fullest human potential.

Another aspect of ministry, of making it with today's people in today's world, is becoming involved in that work, developing skills to do it, and involving others in it. That's not a pattern for predictability; it is a pattern for trustworthiness. And we become trustworthy by trusting.

Trust is putting aside fears, anxieties, suspicions and defense-mechanisms. In the act of trust we accept the goodness and potential of the other. It is a commitment which pushes us beyond our own fear.

The act of trust is not merely a prelude to a new life; it actually causes it. No wonder the teaching and preaching of Christ is so speckled with what is both a warning and an invitation, "Don't be afraid!" He was equipping the people who could help local congregations try to make it with their people in their day.

Angels prepared the way with, "Don't be afraid, Zechariah. God has heard your prayer." And, "Don't be afraid, Mary. God has been gracious to you." And, "Don't be afraid, shepherds. I am here with good news."

And our Lord's own words:

> "Don't be afraid, you are worth more than many sparrows . . .
> "Don't be afraid, father of the dead girl, only believe . . .
> "Don't be afraid, disciples in the boat. It is I . . .
> "Don't be afraid, little flock. Your Father has determined to give you the kingdom . . ."

Christ is with his little flocks, his local congregations and denominations, and the human beings of God everywhere.

And he continues to speak his, "Don't be afraid!"

> Even when we don't know what's going on.
> Even when we don't know where we're going.
> Or what's coming next.

The local congregation has a determined Father and a Friend who is with her.

> Always.
> To the end of the age.
> Don't be afraid!

THE LAST WORD

Can the Church Make It? Still a presumptuous title.

No one I know has the answer to that question in terms of the local congregation.

The effort to respond to the question turned out to be much more "think and do" than "show and tell." It is the effort of one person to say it the way it is, as seen by that one person.

You are called to do your own seeing, telling, thinking, and doing.

A last word: Change and renewal work best when we not only know what we don't want or need anymore, but when we begin to sense what we do need and want. Some aspects of the local congregation's life style can be dropped with few people noticing. Most people are looking for something better, however, not simply for something to be without.

We have advocated friendship instead of authority, human beings of God instead of pre-digested programs, the world around us instead of turned-in self-study, compromise in many areas of thought and action instead of ultimates, small beginnings in place of grandiose dreams, and trust instead of predictability.

None of these is easy. We never said it would be easy.
Nor did he.